Jewish Coloring Book
for Growns Ups

STAR of DAVID

Color for stress relaxation, Jewish meditation,
spiritual renewal, Shabbat peace, and healing

Aliyah Schick

Sacred
Imprints

Other Books by Aliyah Schick

- Jewish Coloring Book: Chai
- Jewish Coloring Book: Alefbet
- Jewish Coloring Book: Judaica
- Meditative Coloring Book 1: Angels
- Meditative Coloring Book 2: Crosses
- Meditative Coloring Book 3: Ancient Symbols
- Meditative Coloring Book 4: Hearts
- Meditative Coloring Book 5: Labyrinths
- Mary Magdalene's Words: Two Women's Spiritual Journey, Both Truth and Fiction, Both Ancient and Now.
- The Mary Magdalene Book

www.JewishColoring.com

Table of Contents

Dedicated to
peaceful moments,
open hearts,
and
self-discovery.

The Star of David Jewish Coloring Book

The *Star of David Jewish Coloring Book for Grown Ups* is much more than a simple coloring book. It is designed to provide you with an easy, creative path for stress reduction, Jewish meditation, spiritual renewal, Shabbat peace, and healing. Color these beautiful drawings and experience your own deep connection to Jewish heritage, community, and *kavannah*.

What Is Jewish Meditation?

We don't usually think of meditation as Jewish. Most people associate the practice with eastern cultures and religions. Consequently, many modern American Jews who are searching for spiritual meaning or mysticism look outside of mainstream Judaism, not realizing the richness already available within our own heritage. In fact, there is a long history of meditation within Judaism, from biblical times all the way to the present.

Just about any form of meditation has been used and is mentioned in ancient Jewish manuscripts, including mantra meditation, contemplation, using phrases and readings, using an idea, a question, or a point of focus, emptying the mind, or using breath or sound. We don't need to adapt eastern forms of meditation, or even to go into esoteric Kabbalistic and Chasidic forms of meditation. There is plenty of room within Reform, Conservative, and Reconstructionist Judaism for authentic Jewish meditation.

Coloring as Meditation

We won't find coloring specifically mentioned in ancient Jewish writings, but it certainly can be meditative, and it can provide focus on our Jewish roots. Whether coloring is approached as relaxation or as a more intentional means for deepening spiritual connection and awareness, meditative coloring allows the mind and body to quiet busyness and overwhelm, and allows understanding, wisdom, and intuition to expand. When focused on Jewish subject matter, coloring easily fits within other forms of Jewish meditation.

History of Jewish Meditation

According to the *Talmud* and *Midrash*, over a million Jews used to study and practice meditation during the time the *Torah* was written. Up until the 19th century there was widespread meditation among Jews. Then during the Jewish Enlightenment of the 1800's, when the intellectual became valued and the mystical denied, anything mystical, including meditation, was put down as superstition and occult. Even the study of *Kabbalah* was intellectualized, and its deeper meanings were lost. Meditation disappeared from Jewish literature by the end of the 19th century, and its earlier value was forgotten.

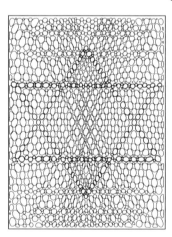

Kavannah

The most common term for meditation in Jewish writings is *kavannah*. From the Hebrew root *kavan*, to aim, *kavannah* means directing your consciousness. Usually translated as concentration, feeling, or devotion, *kavannah* in prayer or worship means allowing the words to bring you to the state of consciousness described in the prayer. In other words, direct your consciousness into a meditative state.

The Amidah

The most commonly used Jewish meditation has always been the daily reciting of the *Amidah*. Most modern Jews don't realize that the *Amidah*, especially the first part, was actually designed as meditation. Repeated three times each day, it is a long mantra, lifting us to a higher level of consciousness. Written 2500 years ago by the Great Assembly during the early years of the Second Temple, the *Amidah* was intended to be a standard meditation for every Jew forever. Its carefully composed words create a resonance that brings the person who recites it close to the divine.

"Ribbono shel Olam"

Another commonly used Jewish mantra is "*Ribbono shel Olam*." This mantra draws our attention to the divine hidden within whatever we are focusing on. The object of attention is then a channel through which we seek and experience the divine. This phrase goes back to biblical times, and was brought to the forefront as a meditation mantra in the early 19th century by Chasidic leader Rabbi Nachman of Bratslav.

The Shema

The *Shema*, Israel's declaration of faith, is to be said twice every day, written in the parchment of the *tefillon* and *mezuzah*, and the last words said before dying. It might seem that the *Shema* would be perfect for a repeating mantra meditation, but the *Talmud* says the *Shema* is not to be used as a repeated mantra. It is meant to be said only once each time. The *shema* could, however, be used in a more fixed, contemplative meditation. Simply focus your entire meditation on the first word, *shema*, and its meaning, "listen" or "hear." Alternatively, contemplate each word, one by one, spending 2 or 3 minutes on each word.

More Information about Jewish Meditation

Within the various historical and present day forms of Jewish meditation there are many possibilities for the modern Jew, whether observant or secular, to find comfortable, effective, and authentically Jewish techniques. For more complete information and specific meditation instructions an excellent resource is the book *Jewish Meditation, A Practical Guide*, by Rabbi Aryeh Kaplan, first published by Schocken Books in 1985.

Making It Yours

Any of these historical forms of Jewish meditation can be combined with coloring to create a meditative practice. You might choose a meaningful mantra word or phrase to repeat silently or softly whisper as you color. Or, begin by reading the weekly Torah portion, then contemplate its message as you color. Or, consider the personal meaning of the drawing's subject matter for you. Put on some beautiful Jewish music, cover your head if that feels right, light candles, wrap yourself in a tallit or shawl, experiment and find what works well for you.

Meditation is very personal, and yet it also connects you with all those millions of Jews, past and present, who have used various forms of meditation to open to and immerse themselves in their faith and culture. Make it yours, and at the same time allow it to deepen your sense of Jewish heritage and belonging.

The Star of David

The six-pointed Star of David is the most familiar Jewish symbol, and it is universally recognized today. Known as the Jewish Star, the *Magen David*, "Star of David," or "Shield of David," this star is often used as a symbol of Judaism and the Jewish people.

Geometry

The Star of David is formed by a geometric shape called a hexagram. It is made of two overlapping, intertwining, equilateral, congruent triangles with the same center point and parallel sides. The center forms a perfect hexagon with six equal sides.

History

The hexagram is rare in early Jewish literature or artwork. The earliest known examples from antiquity include a six-pointed star carved into an archway stone at a 3rd-4th century C.E. synagogue in the Galilee, and another on a 3rd century Jewish tombstone in southern Italy. There are many more examples from the Middle Ages in Jewish manuscripts, on the cover of a *Siddur* (Jewish prayer book), on Jewish flags, and as *segulot* (protective amulets).

In the 14th to 17th centuries the Jews of Prague, Czechoslovakia had their own flag and incorporated the Star of David into it. In the 17th century the Jewish star was often put on the outside of synagogues to identify them, much like a cross would identify a Christian church. By the 19th century the Star of David was commonly used both religiously and secularly to represent the Jewish people, and can be found on tombstones ever since then. In 1897 the early Zionist movement adopted the star as a symbol of the Jewish people, and its use became more popular.

The Star of David is now everywhere Jews are, used as decoration and adornment on both religious and secular items. Find it on a mezuzah, menorah, or tallit bag, on kipot, embroidered on uniforms, tattoos, greeting cards, Shabbat tableware and linens, and on food product packaging. The star is often worn as jewelry, representing Jewish unity and belonging.

The flag of Israel shows a blue Star of David on a white background framed by two horizontal blue stripes. The flag is sometimes called "the flag of Zion." Many Jewish congregations around the world display the Israeli flag in the front of the sanctuary.

A red Star of David is the symbol of Israel's emergency services, the *Magen David Adom*, MDA, equivalent to the U.S. Red Cross and a member of the International Red Cross.

Origins

A Midrash story tells of the teenaged David fighting King Nimrod. During the intense battle the two triangles fastened to the back side of David's round shield to strengthen it became fused together, forming the hexagram Star of David.

The term "Shield of David" was used as early as the 11th century to mean the Holy One, though not associated with the hexagram at that time. This name is used in the *Siddur*, the Jewish prayer book, referring to divine protection of King David. Its meaning as a symbol of the Jewish community may have first developed in the 17th century in Vienna as a boundary marker for the Jewish quarter.

During the Holocaust and World War II the Nazis forced European Jews to wear a yellow Star of David. Then in 1948 the Zionists reclaimed the symbol as one of strength and unity during the founding of the State of Israel, and displayed it proudly on the new national flag.

Meaning

There are many theories about the theological meaning of the Jewish Star. In the Kabbalah the two triangles represent good versus evil or spiritual versus physical. The triangle pointing up indicates our good deeds going up to heaven, and the triangle pointing down is the flow of goodness back down to us.

It has also been said that the two overlapping triangles represent the relationship between the Holy One and the Jewish people. The downward pointing triangle is the divine, reaching down to us, the upward triangle is us here on earth, reaching up to the divine. Or, the twelve sides of the star, created by the six points, can signify the twelve tribes of Israel.

Another idea is that the two triangles symbolize the divisiveness that often arises within the Jewish people, pointing in opposing directions. Or, the intertwining of the triangles makes them inseparable, like the Jewish people.

The center can be seen as solid and substantial, representing the spiritual, while the six points indicate the six universal directions (north, south, east, west, up, and down) into which its influence spreads. Or, the six sides of the center hexagon represent six working days of the week, and the body of the center hexagon is *Shabbat*, the Sabbath.

Symbol of Hope

Many interesting ideas to contemplate! The most important to us in modern times is that the Star of David has become a symbol of Jewish pride in shared heritage, community, and family, and a declaration of hope and commitment.

Suggestions for How to Use This Book

Use this *Jewish Coloring Book* for meditation, spiritual connection, prayer, relaxation, healing, centering, and for coming into your deep, true self. You may simply wish to experience the images in quiet contemplation. Or, you may focus on a Torah portion, a prayer, a phrase, a word, or an affirmation as you work with colors. You may ask for understanding regarding an issue you are dealing with. You may ask for a clearer sense of some aspect of yourself and how it serves you. You may wish to experience a deeper sense of your Jewish heritage and faith. You may wish to cover your head or wrap yourself in a tallit or shawl.

Open your heart and your mind as you use this *Jewish Coloring Book*. Pay attention to impressions and ideas, feelings, intuition, and messages. They may very well be exactly what you need to hear.

Tools
Choose your favorite coloring tools, or you might like to gather a variety of pens, crayons, colored pencils, chalk, oil pastels, markers, glitter pens, paints, etc. You may want to place a blank sheet of paper behind the page so ink or paint does not go through.

Music
Consider playing background music as you color. Try soft instrumental, a heartfelt Jewish singer, or even Klezmer for a more lively experience.

Nature
Sometimes a favorite spot outdoors provides just the right environment for meditation, coloring, and creative expression. Beach, woods, backyard, porch, treehouse, mountain top, stream, pond, park, etc.

Silence
You may prefer quiet, so that all your attention focuses on what you are doing. Emptiness can give rise to profound experience.

Meditation
You may like to meditate first, and then begin working with the colors. Try any of the many ways of meditation, or simply be with your breath for a few minutes, following it in and out. Or, you may wish to try the following meditation. Read it silently or out loud, slowly, pausing to draw in each breath.

A *Ruach* (Breathing) Meditation

• Take in a breath... and on the exhale release the day's happenings, settling into this peaceful time of creative, spiritual connection.

• Take in a breath... and on the exhale let go of worries and troubles and burdens. You can pick them up again later if you need to.

• Take in a breath... and on the exhale come into the center of your Self. From there drop a line down through your body, through the chair and the floor and into the earth. Through soil and sand and stone, through coal and underground stream, and minerals and precious metals. Down through all the colors and textures and densities of the earth, down into the hot magma at this planet's core. Down to the very center of earth and center of the essence of physical being. Tie your line there. Anchor yourself there.

• Take in a breath... and on the exhale extend your line up from your center, through your body and out the crown of your head, up through the ceiling, the roof, and into the sky. Past clouds and wind and thinning gases, out through the atmosphere and into space. Past the sun and galaxy and stars and universe, out to the depths of the source of all that is. Feel your connection there. You are part of the great cosmos. You are one with all being.

• Take in a breath... and on the exhale return to the drawing before you and ask that you be open to receiving guidance and understanding as you spend time with it. Know that there are no mistakes, only new choices and combinations and patterns that suggest new perception at an other-than-conscious level. Or that remind us of something that can now be released. Or that create an opening to new possibilities.

• Take in a breath... and on the exhale release "shoulds" and rules and expectations. Let go and open to new possibilities.

• Now, begin by picking up whatever color catches your attention.

About the Artist

Aliyah Schick has been an artist all of her life. After Peace Corps in the Andes Mountains of South America, she studied art full time for four years, then created and sold pottery and ceramic art pieces for many years. Later Aliyah worked in fiber and fabric, making soft sculptural wall pieces and art quilts, then fabric dolls designed to carry healing energy. Now she draws and paints, and she writes poems and prose.

At the heart of all this, Aliyah's passion is healing. She is a skilled and dynamic deep energetic healer and Transformation Coach. Her work in the multidimensional layers and patterns of the auric field is powerful and effective. Her drawings, paintings, poetry, writings, and books all arise as expressions of Aliyah's healing abilities. Spending time with these drawings serves to remind us who we are, where we come from, and why we are here.

Aliyah lives and works in the beautiful Blue Ridge Mountains of North Carolina, where the energy of the earth is easily accessible, ancient, motherly, and obvious. A place where people speak with familiarity and reverence of the land and spirit, and where the sacred comes to sit with us on the porch to share the afternoon sun.

www.AliyahSchick.com

The
Drawings

Opposite each drawing is a blank page for your

Notes & Impressions

Use these pages to catch and keep hold of thoughts, wishes, intentions, affirmations, prayers, poems, memories, notes, drawings, or whatever comes to you as you explore coloring with this book. Make it yours.

15

17

19

21

23

27

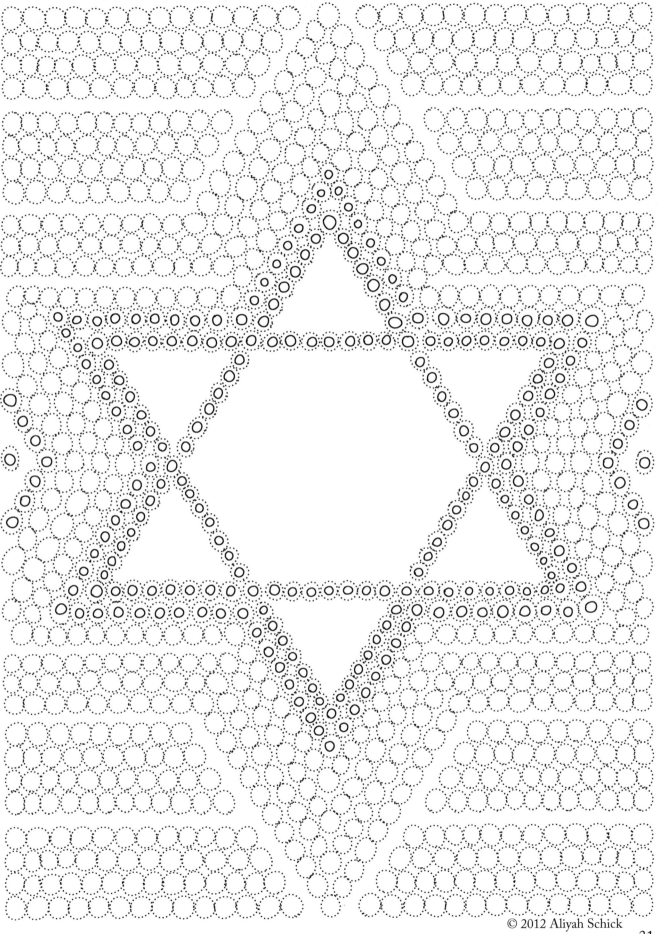

33

35

© 2012 Aliyah Schick

39

45

47

49

51

53

55

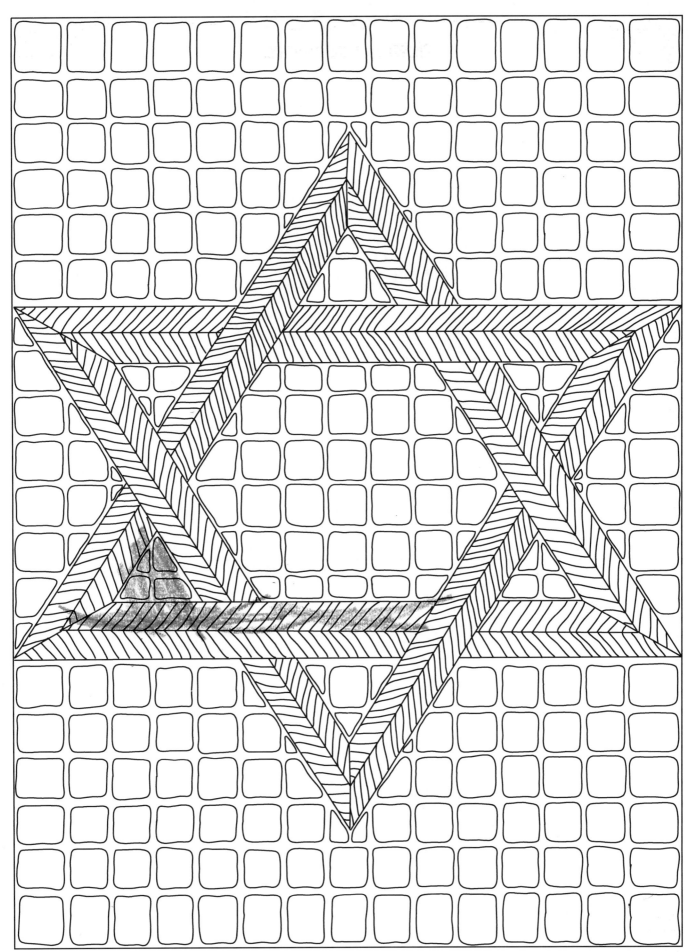

61

63

67

© 2012 Aliyah Schick

73

75

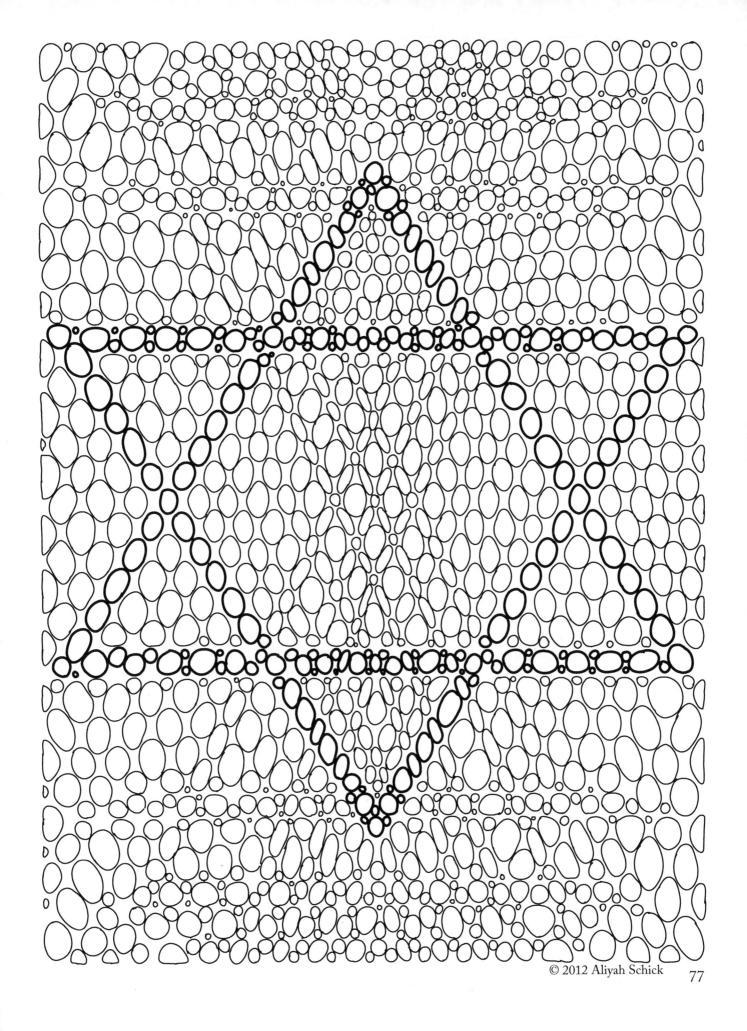

77

79

81

83

85

The Jewish Coloring Books for Grown Ups

Color for stress relaxation, Jewish meditation, Shabbat peace, and healing.

CHAI Coloring Book

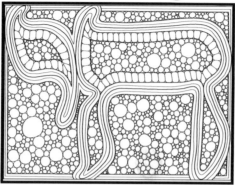

The Jewish *Chai* symbol represents the Hebrew word *chai*, meaning life. It is worn, displayed, or given as a gift as a symbol and reminder of the Jewish love for life, to celebrate being Jewish, and to bring abundant good luck. The *Chai Jewish Coloring Book for Grown Ups* offers you the opportunity to spend relaxed, meditative time immersed in the joy of the *Chai*.

STAR OF DAVID Coloring Book

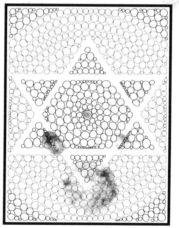

The six-pointed Star of David is our most familiar Jewish symbol. Used as decoration and adornment on both religious and secular items, and often worn as jewelry, the Star of David represents Jewish pride in shared heritage, community, and family, and a declaration of hope and commitment. Spend some time coloring these drawings of the Star of David as a means to allow yourself to ground into your Jewish roots.

The Jewish Coloring Books for Grown Ups

Color for stress relaxation, Jewish meditation, Shabbat peace, and healing.

ALEFBET Coloring Book

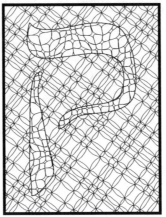

Alef, bet, gimel, dalet, hey, vav, zayin, chet, tet, yod, kaf, lamed, mem, nun, samech, ayin, peh, tsade, qof, resh, shin, and tav; 22 letters in the Hebrew Alefbet. Coloring these beautiful drawings based on the Hebrew letter forms is relaxing, reduces stress, and lightens your load, as it connects you with your Jewish roots. These letters are said to be the building blocks of the universe. Spending peaceful time coloring them can be beneficial in more deeply healing ways, too.

JUDAICA Coloring Book

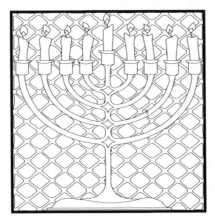

Menorah, dredel, Ten Commandment tablets, challah, Torah scrolls, Magen David, Havdalah braid, mezuzah, and more. Color these beautiful drawings based on familiar Jewish objects and symbols. Relax, unwind, de-stress, and allow healing as you ground yourself into your Jewish heritage. L'chaim!

The Meditative Coloring Books Series:
Angels, Crosses, Ancient Symbols, Hearts, and Labyrinths

Meditative Coloring Book 1 -- Angels

Artist Aliyah Schick draws these angelic images within a meditation. With a pen in each hand, she allows the lines to go where they will, as the two sides mirror each other. Every movement is guided by spirit; every drawing is different; and each one is a wonderful surprise filled with angelic presence.

Meditative Coloring Book 2 -- Crosses

The cross is one of the most ancient and enduring sacred symbols, found in nearly every culture from cave dwellers throughout human existence. It symbolizes the celestial, spiritual divine coming into being in this material world. It represents the sacred taking form, and the integration of soul into physical life. The drawings of the Crosses Series feature ancient and contemporary images of the cross in reflections of the deep spiritual significance of its form.

---

www.MeditativeColoring.com

Meditative Coloring Book 3 -- Ancient Symbols

Ancient and indigenous sacred images speak deeply to us, to our bellies and our bones, to our cellular memory and our wisdom, to our souls' yearnings. Native peoples throughout time and place see the sacred in all of life. For them, holiness is life and life is holiness. Life is the manifestation of the holy in all things. The drawings of the Ancient Symbols Series feature timeless designs used by every culture on earth to remind us of the sacred.

Meditative Coloring Book 4 -- Hearts

The heart is one of our favorite symbols, evoking feelings of love, caring, loyalty, and devotion. As you spend time with these Sacred Imprints Heart drawings, open your heart to live with more compassion for others and for yourself. Open your life to deeper connection with the earth and all of life. Open yourself to recognize the sacred in all things, including in yourself.

Meditative Coloring Book 5 -- Labyrinths

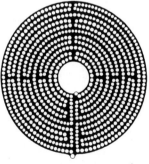

These original artist's labyrinth drawings invite you to color your steps into the labyrinth, one by one, as you contemplate, meditate, or pray. Go deep into your inner wisdom and guidance where questions' answers reveal themselves and choices come clear. Or simply relax and be with your breathing. Now you can bring your labyrinth with you to wherever you need to be.

Sacred Imprints

Made in the USA
Middletown, DE
20 March 2016